Feline Friends

Columbus, OH • Chicago, IL • Redmond, WA

The **McGraw·Hill** Companies

The Independent Reading Books

The *Independent Reading Books* are reading books that fill the need for easy-to-read stories for the primary grades. The appeal of these stories will encourage independent reading at the early grade levels.

The stories focus on the Dolch 220 Basic Sight Vocabulary and the 95 Common Nouns. Beyond these lists, the books use about three new words per page.

This series was prepared under the direction and supervision of Edward W. Dolch, Ph.D.

This revision was prepared under the direction and supervision of Eleanor Dolch LaRoy and the Dolch Family Trust.

SRAonline.com

 SRA

Send all inquiries to:
SRA/McGraw-Hill
8787 Orion Place
Columbus, OH 43240-4027

Printed in the United States of America.

ISBN 0-07-602514-4

3 4 5 6 7 8 9 BSF 12 11 10 09 08 07 06 05

The **McGraw·Hill** Companies

Table of Contents

Jasper, Come Back

Mr. Lafontaine and his family were going from New York to St. Louis. The children, Muriel and Claude, were in the back of the car with Jasper, a big black-and-white cat.

The car was going down a road when a big truck that was on Mr. Lafontaine's side of the road came at them. Mr. Lafontaine turned the car off on his side of the road. The truck did not hit the car.

Everything happened so fast. Jasper, the big black-and-white cat, jumped out of the open car window and ran away into the woods as fast as he could go.

Muriel and Claude got out of the car and ran after Jasper calling, "Jasper, Jasper, come back!" But Jasper ran on and on.

Mr. and Mrs. Lafontaine got out of the car and went into the woods calling, "Jasper, come back!" But they could not find Jasper.

The family got back into the car. The children wanted to keep looking for Jasper because they loved him very much.

"We will have to go on to St. Louis," said Mr. Lafontaine. "I have work to do there, and I must be there today."

Mrs. Lafontaine said, "Soon we will be going back to New York on this road. We will stop and look for Jasper again."

Mrs. Lafontaine said to Mr. Lafontaine, "I don't think we will ever see Jasper again."

When the family got to St. Louis, Mr. Lafontaine went to work. Mrs. Lafontaine and the children had a good time in the city. But Muriel and Claude were always thinking about Jasper.

When Mr. Lafontaine was done with his work, the family got into the car and started back to New York. Pretty soon Claude called out, "This is where Jasper ran away."

Mr. Lafontaine stopped the car. There on the side of the road sat a black-and-white cat. It was Jasper.

4

Mr. Lafontaine opened the car door, and the children jumped out. Jasper ran and jumped into the car. He had found his family.

There are many stories about cats that somehow find their way home after they have run away. But Jasper was a cat that did not try to find his way home, because his family found him.

Tempest, the Actor

Tempest lived in a theater. He was loved by all the people at the theater. The actors thought it was good to have Tempest live in the theater.

One night Tempest walked into a play onstage. He walked out and sat down in front of the fireplace on the stage.

The actors on the stage were very surprised, but they went on with the play.

Tempest just sat in front of the fireplace. He washed one paw and then the other paw.

At the end of the play when the curtain came down, the people in the audience clapped and clapped. The actors went in front of the curtain as the audience clapped.

The director of the play gave Tempest to an actor, and she took him in front of the curtain. How the audience clapped for the new actor!

That is how Tempest got to be an actor.

The director of the play knew that somehow he must get Tempest to be in the play every night. People liked to see a cat in the play sitting in front of the fireplace.

The next day no one could get Tempest to sit in front of the stage fireplace and wash his paws. The director did not know what to do.

Then the boy who took care of Tempest said, "Tempest is a good cat, but he does not know how to be an actor. He just knows how to catch mice. If I had a mouse, I could get Tempest to sit in front of the fireplace."

"We will get a mouse for Tempest," said the director. "Try to get Tempest to sit in front of the fireplace."

The boy made a little opening in the stage fireplace. Every night he would get in back of the fireplace with a mouse in a cage. Tempest sat in front of the fireplace watching the mouse. Tempest thought he was going to catch that mouse.

One night the mouse got away. It ran onstage. An actor onstage who was afraid of mice did not think at all about the play and jumped up on a chair. The curtain had to come down. The audience laughed.

Every night Tempest sat by the stage fireplace and watched that mouse, but he never caught it.

Tempest was glad when the play ended. He would sleep in his box at the back of the theater. At night, when no one was in the theater, Tempest caught mice.

The Green Parrot

Once there was a French cat. Her owner was a writer. The cat would always sit with the man when he would write books.

She was a curious cat. She followed her owner when he walked in the garden. She sat on a chair by the table. The man and the cat ate together. Her name was Madam.

One day a friend of the writer came to see him. "I am going away, and I don't know what to do with my parrot when I am away," said the friend.

"I will keep your parrot for you," said the writer.

"This is very good of you," said the friend, "but my parrot talks a lot. She could keep you from doing your work."

"I know that a parrot will not keep me from doing my work," said the writer.

So the pretty green parrot came to live in the house with Madam.

Madam was surprised to see this strange-looking bird. All day long Madam sat and watched the parrot in its cage. Madam was a very curious cat.

She must have thought this strange-looking bird was some kind of a green chicken. Madam knew that chickens were good to eat. How could she get this green chicken out of its cage?

The parrot was very afraid. She knew the cat was thinking that a bird is good to eat. The parrot sat in her cage and looked down at Madam.

Madam walked around and around the cage that hung on a stand. Madam's tail went from side to side. She was very curious.

Just as Madam was about to jump at the cage, the parrot cried in a loud voice, "Have you had your breakfast? Have you had your breakfast?"

The cat was never so surprised in all her life. She stopped and looked at the parrot. This green chicken talked like a person.

Then the parrot said in a loud voice, "What did you have for breakfast?"

"This is not a bird," thought Madam. "This green chicken is a strange person."

Madam looked at the writer. He was laughing. Madam did not want to be laughed at, so she ran under the bed and stayed there all day.

From that day on, Madam had little to do with the green chicken that talked like a person.

Nina

Mr. Petroff had a restaurant. He was a kind man, and everyone who worked in the restaurant liked Mr. Petroff.

One day Mr. Petroff opened the back door, and there was a big striped cat looking for something to eat. No one who was hungry was ever turned away from Mr. Petroff's restaurant. So Mr. Petroff put food and water beside the back door for the cat.

Before Mr. Petroff went home that night, he looked out the back door of his restaurant. The big striped cat was in a box beside the door.

The cat was in the box with three little kittens. She meowed and purred and showed Mr. Petroff her three striped kittens.

"I am going to call you Nina," said Mr. Petroff. "Mrs. Petroff is called Nina, and she is just as proud of our three children as you are of your kittens."

From that time on, Nina, the striped cat, lived in a box at the back door of Mr. Petroff's restaurant. There was always a dish of food and a dish of water for her.

Once some dogs wanted to eat Nina's food, but she soon made them see that they had to keep away from Mr. Petroff's restaurant.

One morning Mr. Petroff looked in the box to see the kittens. He saw five kittens in the box. One was white, one was black, and three were striped.

"Nina, Nina," said Mr. Petroff, "where did you get that white kitten and that black kitten?"

Nina just meowed and purred. She did not tell Mr. Petroff where she had found the white kitten and the black kitten.

"Nina," said Mr. Petroff, "you will have to have a bigger box for a bigger family."

Every day Mr. Petroff put a bigger dish of food and a bigger dish of water outside the back door of his restaurant.

Very soon Nina brought home a yellow kitten. Then there were six kittens in the big box. Nina liked to have many kittens in the box with her.

There was always a dish of food and a dish of water for the growing family. Nina washed her kittens and took good care of them. When the kittens got big, they got

out of the box and played around the back door of Mr. Petroff's restaurant.

Nina made a good home for her family of kittens.

Nina would always look for kittens. When she got home, she was carrying a kitten in her mouth. No one knew where Nina found the kittens, but the kittens were always hungry.

Soon Mr. Petroff saw that there were many kittens in the big box beside the back door of his restaurant.

"Nina," said Mr. Petroff, "I never thought I would have food for so many kittens. But if you can take care of all these kittens, I think I can give them food."

Mr. Petroff put a bigger dish of food and a bigger dish of water outside the back door of his restaurant.

When Nina's kittens got big, she always found some baby kittens to bring back to her big box beside Mr. Petroff's back door.

Ko's Gifts

There are many stories about cats that take gifts to their owners. Some cats get mice and bring them to their owners. Some cats bring baby rabbits or baby birds to their owners and then want their owners to look after the baby animals.

One cat brought food to his owner. His owner never knew where the cat got the fish he put at her feet. The cat never ate any of the food.

Ko was a Siamese cat, and he loved his owner, April, very much. Ko liked to go to other houses in the neighborhood. Whenever Ko saw something he thought his owner would like, he picked it up in his mouth and carried it home. He brought April a newspaper. He brought her some ribbon too.

Ko's owner was always trying to find the owners of the gifts Ko brought her. April could not stop Ko from bringing her things from other people in the neighborhood. Ko thought his owner would like his gifts.

One day Ko took a ball of yellow yarn and brought it to April. April thought that someone could be knitting a sweater and would want the ball of yellow yarn. She looked but could not find anyone in the neighborhood who was knitting a yellow sweater.

The next day Ko took a sleeve that was made from the yellow yarn and brought it to April. April talked to Ko, but Ko could not tell her where he found the sleeve made of yellow yarn.

Ko must have thought April liked the yellow yarn because the next day Ko took all of the sweater and brought it home. April saw that the yarn was on the sweater. The yarn went over her backyard fence and into the next yard.

April took the ball of yarn, the sweater, and the sleeve and followed the yarn over the back fence. She went into the next yard and down the street. She did not know how Ko had carried the sweater so far. She followed the yarn a long way. She came to a backyard where she found the end of the yellow yarn.

The woman in that house said she had been knitting a yellow sweater in the backyard. She went into the house but did not take the yellow sweater with her.

The woman laughed when she found out about Ko. She said to April, "You must make a yellow sweater, too, and then your cat will stay at home with you."

Rusty

Rusty was a beautiful yellow cat. One day he walked into a big hotel in New York City. Rusty lived in that hotel from that day on.

Everyone in the hotel loved Rusty. Mr. Case, the hotel owner, lived in an apartment on the tenth floor. This was Rusty's home.

Rusty went up and down in the elevator. When the elevator got to the tenth floor, he got out of the elevator and walked to Mr. Case's apartment. Then he meowed at Mr. Case's apartment door. Rusty always went to the right door.

Going down the elevator, Rusty sometimes stopped at the fourth floor. On the fourth floor lived a man who knew much about cats. This man made friends with Rusty. He always had some fish for Rusty.

Only once did Rusty ever get off the elevator at any floor but the lobby floor, the tenth floor, or the fourth floor.

One day Rusty went down to the lobby on the first floor of the hotel. He liked to watch the people, and he liked to sleep in one of the chairs.

A French poodle came into the hotel lobby with his owner. This dog did not like cats. As soon as the poodle came into the lobby, he saw Rusty. The poodle was such a big dog that his owner could not hold him back. Before anyone knew what had happened, the big French poodle had Rusty in his mouth.

Everyone in the lobby ran around and made a lot of noise. But no one could make the big French poodle put Rusty down.

Then a man put water on the dog's nose. That made the big dog open his mouth, and Rusty ran away as fast as he could go.

An elevator door was open. Rusty ran into the elevator. He and a man in the elevator went to the tenth floor where Rusty lived.

This time Rusty did not get off at the tenth floor. He just sat in the back of the elevator with big frightened eyes. Rusty did not get out of the elevator until it got to the top floor. Then the cat got out and ran away.

Rusty stayed on the top floor of the hotel for four days. Then he got hungry and went down to his home on the tenth floor.

Charles

Charles was a Siamese cat. He made a lot of noise when he purred, and he meowed in a loud voice, as many Siamese cats do.

Charles was very smart and very curious. When he was a kitten, he wanted to learn everything at once. He ran all over the house. He knocked things down. His owner had to put all his pretty things away.

Charles climbed the curtains. But his owner only laughed and said, "Charles, you will have to grow up and be a good cat."

Charles was curious about the water in the bathroom. He thought it was very funny. He watched it with big blue eyes, but he did not want any water on him.

There were two things Charles did not like at all: the vacuum cleaner and firecrackers. The vacuum cleaner made such a funny noise. Charles would run

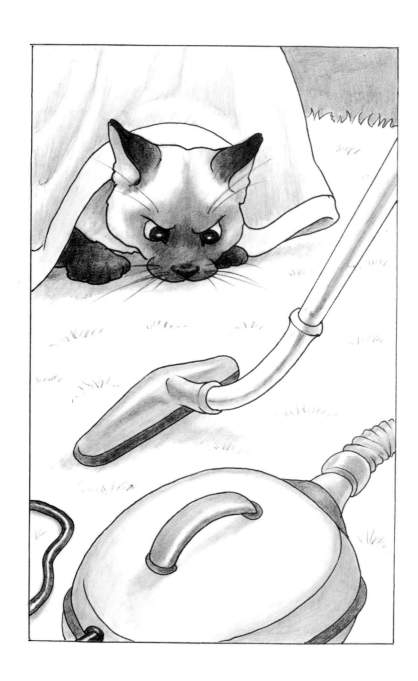

under the bed whenever he saw the vacuum cleaner.

Charles did not like firecrackers. He was always surprised at what a loud noise those little firecrackers made.

Charles was curious about Rupert, the canary. Rupert lived in a cage. The cage hung on a stand. Charles sat and looked up at Rupert. He wanted to see the bird better. Day after day he jumped at Rupert's cage, but he could not get the canary.

One day Charles gave a big jump and hit the stand. Over went the stand, and down went the cage to the floor.

Charles sat on the floor by the cage and looked at Rupert. He did not try to hurt the canary. After that, Rupert's cage was hung where Charles could not get at it.

Charles was never again curious about birds. When he played outside, he never wanted to catch birds.

Charles did not want to fight other cats. Once, a big cat hurt Charles, but Charles would not fight back. He ran to his owner.

Charles went everywhere with his owner, who was a soldier. He went in airplanes, on trains, in cars, and in trucks. He went from camp to camp. The soldiers at the camps loved Charles and gave him good things to eat.

Once his owner was not well and had to go to the hospital for soldiers. Charles went to the hospital too. He stayed in the hospital with his owner until his owner got well.

Panther Is a Hero

Mrs. Yashima did not live with anyone—
that is, anyone but Panther. Panther was a
big black cat and a very smart cat.

Panther knew just when Mrs. Yashima
wanted to get up in the morning. He would
jump on her bed and put his paw on her
face until she opened her eyes.

Mrs. Yashima said that Panther got
her up every morning. She did not know
how the cat knew when to get her up.

One night Panther jumped on Mrs. Yashima's bed and patted her face with his paw. Mrs. Yashima made Panther jump off the bed.

"It is not morning, Panther. It is night. It is not time to play. Go to sleep."

Panther jumped up on the bed again. He meowed and meowed in such a strange way that Mrs. Yashima got out of bed.

"What is it, Panther? Do you want to go outside?"

Mrs. Yashima did not want to get out of bed, but she got up and turned on the light. Panther ran to the door and looked back at Mrs. Yashima and meowed in a strange way.

"Yes, Panther," said Mrs. Yashima. "I will let you outside."

Then Mrs. Yashima heard someone call her name. Someone knocked and knocked on the front door.

Mrs. Yashima knew something was not right. She ran to the door. She saw that the house was on fire.

Mrs. Yashima opened the front door, and a neighbor said, "I am so glad you are not sleeping. I have called the firefighters. They will be here right away." So Mrs. Yashima and Panther ran to the neighbor's house.

The firefighters came at once and saved the little house.

"Panther saved my life," said Mrs. Yashima to her neighbors. "I was asleep. I am afraid that I would have been hurt if Panther had not jumped on my bed and patted my face."

Mrs. Yashima told the newspaper how Panther had saved her life and saved her house. The newspaper printed the story.

People from all over the city went to the little house to see Panther. They called him a hero.

Mrs. Yashima and Panther lived together for a long time. And every morning the big black cat got his owner up. He jumped on her bed and patted her face with his paw until she opened her eyes.

Phantom Liked to Fish

Cats like to eat fish, but not many cats catch their own fish.

There was a cat in Florida who lived in a small hotel by the ocean. People from the city stayed at this hotel so they could go fishing on the pier that went out into the ocean.

In the morning this big gray cat followed the people out to the pier. He would sit beside them until someone caught a fish for him.

As soon as the fish was put down on the pier for him, the cat would take it in his mouth and run to the cook at the hotel. The cook always cooked the fish and gave it to the cat.

The people said it was good to have the cat there because they always caught fish when the big gray cat was on the pier. The cat's name was Phantom.

But the big gray cat was a fisherman too. His owner, who was a fisherman, told the people about Phantom.

"Once, when Phantom was a little kitten, I took him to the ocean. He liked the water so much that he jumped in the ocean.

"Then I took Phantom out with me in my fishing boat. When Phantom was with me, I always thought I caught many fish.

"Phantom was a good cat on the boat," said the fisherman. "He would take a fish only when I gave it to him. He would stand in the front of the fishing boat and look down into the water.

"One day, I ran into a school of fish. There were fish all around the boat. Phantom jumped into the water. He caught a fish in his mouth.

"Phantom looked funny. He was carrying the fish in his mouth.

"I got Phantom out of the water and into the boat. From that time on, he caught his own fish."

The people from the city always wanted to get Phantom to go out on the pier with them. They thought they would catch many fish if Phantom sat beside them. Phantom was a fisherman, but he liked to let the people from the city catch fish for him.

Grandmother's Chair

Grandmother liked to sit by the window in a rocking chair. No other person in the family sat in this chair.

"It is Grandmother's chair," said Carlos.

"It is Grandmother's chair," said Isabella.

But Mimado, the big striped cat, thought Grandmother's chair was his chair. If Grandmother was not sitting in her chair, Mimado jumped into the rocking chair and went to sleep.

"Look at Mimado," said Carlos. "He is asleep in Grandmother's rocking chair."

Grandmother laughed when she saw Mimado asleep in her chair.

"You look comfortable, Mimado," said Grandmother. "I will sit in this chair until you are done sleeping."

One day Grandmother was sitting in her rocking chair when Mimado came into the house. Mimado looked at Grandmother a long time. Grandmother was reading a book and did not look at Mimado.

Mimado meowed and walked around Grandmother's chair. Mimado could not get Grandmother to understand that he wanted to sleep in her rocking chair.

So the big cat went to sleep at her feet, and she went on reading her book.

Mimado opened his eyes and looked at Grandmother. Sleeping on the floor was not as comfortable as sleeping in Grandmother's chair. Mimado went to the door and meowed.

"Yes," said Grandmother, as she put down her book. "You are a good cat and always ask to go outside. I will let you go out."

Grandmother went to the door and opened it, but Mimado did not go outside. He turned, jumped into Grandmother's rocking chair, and went to sleep.

Grandmother laughed and laughed. She called Carlos and Isabella and told them what Mimado had done.

"Mimado is a smart cat," said Grandmother. "I think I will let him sleep in my comfortable rocking chair."

Pansy

Pansy lived in a big city. As a kitten, Pansy liked to walk the streets of the city.

Pansy learned how to keep away from people's feet. She learned how not to get run over by cars. When evening came, Pansy always went home for supper. She was always hungry.

Pansy was a very beautiful cat. Because she walked the streets of the big city, her owner, Mr. Joseph, was afraid something would happen to Pansy. City streets are no place for a beautiful cat.

One evening Pansy did not come home for supper. Mr. Joseph called and called for her, but she did not come.

The next day Pansy did not come home. Mr. Joseph called and called again, but Pansy did not come home. Mr. Joseph was thinking that something had happened to Pansy. Mr. Joseph loved his cat.

Mr. Joseph had signs printed. The signs said that Pansy was a beautiful black-and-white cat. Mr. Joseph said that anyone who brought Pansy home would get a dollar.

He put the printed signs on fences and in apartments.

That evening a little boy and his father came to see their neighbor, Mr. Joseph. The boy told Mr. Joseph he had seen Pansy in a backyard.

The sun was going down, so Mr. Joseph got a light. Mr. Joseph and his neighbors went into many backyards. They did find a little kitten in a box, but the cat was not Pansy.

Mr. Joseph gave the boy a dollar and thanked him for telling about the cat that was in the backyard.

The next morning, two boys came to Mr. Joseph's door. One little boy carried a black cat, and the other carried a white cat.

"Which cat is Pansy?" asked the boys.

"No, no," said Mr. Joseph. "Pansy is a black-and-white cat." Then he said, "Thank you for trying to find Pansy for me." He gave the boys their dollars.

The next child brought a yellow cat to Mr. Joseph.

"Is this cat Pansy?" asked the child.

"No, no," said Mr. Joseph. "The signs said that Pansy is a black-and-white cat." Then he gave the child a dollar.

Some children found out that Mr. Joseph would give a dollar if they would bring cats to him. They thought this was a good way to get a dollar.

All day long children brought cats to Mr. Joseph. There were little cats and big cats. There were gray cats and striped cats. There were black cats and white cats. But not one child found Pansy.

Mr. Joseph did not know what to do.
He could not give money to the children
any longer when they brought him cats.

Mr. Joseph was thinking he would
never see Pansy again. But one evening

Pansy came home for supper. She never told Mr. Joseph where she had been.

Mr. Joseph laughed when he saw Pansy. "You pretty cat," said Mr. Joseph. "I gave away a lot of money for you, but I am glad you came home."

That Kitten

Mai Ling is a Siamese kitten. She is pretty, and she is smart. Mai Ling lives with the Davises, and she runs the house.

All Siamese cats like to climb, and Mai Ling likes to climb all kinds of things. She climbs up people's legs so she can sit with them. She climbs up curtains, but when she gets to the ceiling, Mai Ling gets frightened. She puts out all her claws, and she tears the curtains as she comes down from the ceiling.

Mr. Davis has a dog named Hero. Hero thought he would run Mai Ling out of the house. Hero is ten times as big as Mai Ling.

When Mr. Davis first got Mai Ling, he thought Hero would hurt the kitten. But Mai Ling faced Hero. She jumped at his nose with all her claws out. Now Hero runs away from Mai Ling.

Mai Ling looks all over the house for Hero. When she finds him asleep, the kitten jumps on his head. Before Hero knows what is happening, Mai Ling runs away and goes under a chair where Hero cannot get her. If Hero puts his head under the chair to look for Mai Ling, she hits his nose with her claws.

At night Mai Ling jumps on the bed where Mr. Davis is sleeping. He must be very still so Mai Ling will go to sleep and not play as if she has found a mouse.

Mai Ling likes to sit in the bathroom and put her paw into the water. She cannot understand where the water comes from.

One of the things she likes best is to watch Mr. Davis every morning. She sits and watches him with her big blue eyes.

In the bathroom Mai Ling finds many things to climb. One morning when Mr. Davis was shaving, Mai Ling jumped

up on the window curtain. The kitten climbed until she got to the ceiling. Then she looked down. The white tub was under her. It was a long way down.

Mai Ling was frightened. She cried and cried. Mr. Davis went on with his shaving. Mai Ling wanted to turn around, but the claws that had helped her climb up the curtain did not help her climb down the curtain.

Mai Ling was very frightened. She cried and cried. Mai Ling cried out in such a loud voice that Mrs. Davis ran into the bathroom.

"Mai Ling, come down from that window curtain," said Mrs. Davis.

The kitten jumped from the window curtain onto the shower curtain. Now, shower curtains are not made for kittens' claws because their claws will tear the curtains. Well, Mai Ling tore the shower curtain.

Mrs. Davis picked up Mai Ling and said, "Pretty soon Mai Ling will grow up to be a mother cat. Then she will not tear shower curtains."

Mr. Davis was done shaving now, and he said to Mrs. Davis, "Yes, Mai Ling will be a mother cat one day, and she will have little kittens. They will be as pretty and as smart as Mai Ling. What will Hero and I do then?"

Socks Is Lost

The Smith family was in their kitchen. They were all around the kitchen table. Mother and Father were there. The boys, Scott and Hank, were at the long table. So were the girls, Judy and Samantha. Everyone in the family was in the kitchen, but one. Socks was not there! Where was Socks?

Socks was the family cat. Mother and Father loved Socks. The children did too. He had been in the family for a long, long time. But now the Smiths did not know where Socks was.

"We must find Socks," Mother said. "First let's look for Socks in the house."

Scott went up to look in his room. He looked under the chair. Socks was not there. Then he looked under the coat that was on the chair. No Socks! He called out for Socks, but the little cat was not there.

Hank looked in his room too. He looked under the bed and behind the door, but he did not find Socks. He called out for Socks, too, but the little cat was not there.

Judy looked for Socks in her room. She looked behind some books that were on the floor, but Socks was not there. She called out for Socks, but the little cat was not there.

Samantha went up to look in her room for Socks. She looked behind her door. Was that a tail behind her toys? It looked just like Socks's tail! Samantha took a better look. No, it was not Socks. It was her toy dog.

Father went up to look in his and Mother's room. He looked all around the room. He looked behind the door, under the bed, under the chair, and under the table. But no Socks.

Everyone looked in all the other rooms in the house, but they could not find Socks. The family came back to the kitchen. They knew they had to keep looking.

"Where is Socks?" asked the children. "We want to find Socks."

"I will look outside," said Mother.

Mother went out into the yard. She walked around the yard looking for Socks. Mother looked in the trees and in the yard next door. Mother looked by the birds' nest, and she looked by the family car. But she could not find Socks.

Mother went back into the kitchen. "I cannot find Socks in the yard," she said. "I just don't know where he could be."

"Well, I would like a drink of water," said Father. "All this looking has made me thirsty."

"I am thirsty too, Father," said Hank. "May I have a drink of water?"

"Everyone who is thirsty put up your hand," said Father. All the children put up their hands.

Father opened the cupboard door to find something for everyone to drink out of. And just as he opened the door, out jumped Socks!

"Socks!" all the children cried out. "Socks was in the cupboard!"

"Look, children," said Father. "I found Socks!"

Socks was so glad to be out of the cupboard. He looked up at everyone. He meowed and meowed. It was as if he were saying, "Thank you for finding me."

Everyone sat down at the kitchen table and laughed about finding Socks in the kitchen cupboard.

Cat Tricks

Kevin Young had a TV show about animals. Kevin liked all animals. But of all the animals, Kevin liked cats best. So once, the show was just about cats.

"On today's show," said Kevin, "we have three children and their cats. These cats do funny tricks. First here is Andrew White and his cat."

"I am Andrew White, and this is my cat, Jinx," said the boy.

"So Andrew, show us what kind of tricks Jinx can do," said Kevin.

Andrew put Jinx on top of Kevin's table and told the cat to sit. Jinx did sit! Kevin laughed.

"That is only one of Jinx's tricks. Watch this," said Andrew.

Andrew had a little silver toy car that he showed to Jinx. Jinx watched as Andrew put the silver toy car in his hand.

Andrew said, "Kevin, please clap your hands."

At the noise of the clap, Jinx jumped from the table, up onto Andrew's back, and then up onto Andrew's head! Then Jinx jumped down from Andrew's head onto his hand and knocked the silver toy car out of Andrew's hand. Andrew caught the car with his other hand.

"That is one of the best tricks I have seen," laughed Kevin. "And all I did was clap my hands! Thank you for showing us Jinx's tricks."

Andrew White and Jinx sat on a chair by the table to watch the show.

"Now here is Sally Chapman and her cat," said Kevin as a girl walked in.

"I am Sally Chapman, and this is my cat, Rings," she said.

"Tell us what Rings does," said Kevin.

"Rings plays a drum," said Sally.

Sally put a little drum on the table. Then she put Rings on the table next to the drum.

"Drum!" Sally said to Rings.

Rings turned around and started to hit the drum with his tail. His tail flew up and down on the drum. It flew faster and faster.

This made a lot of noise! Kevin was laughing, and so was everyone watching the show.

"That is also one of the best tricks I have seen," said Kevin.

Sally Chapman and Rings sat on a chair next to Andrew White and Jinx to watch the show.

"Now here is Cindy Pettigo and her cat," said Kevin as a girl walked in.

"I am Cindy Pettigo. This is my cat, Princess," said the girl.

"Cindy, please show us what Princess can do," said Kevin.

Cindy put Princess on the table and took out a small silver spoon. When Princess saw the silver spoon, her eyes got big. As Cindy moved the spoon around, Princess watched it. When Cindy moved the spoon up, Princess looked up. When Cindy moved the spoon down, Princess looked down.

Cindy put the spoon on the end of the table. Princess hit the spoon with her paw. The spoon flew up over the table. When the spoon came down, Princess caught it with her mouth.

"What a trick," said Kevin, and he clapped his hands.

When Kevin clapped his hands, Jinx jumped out of Andrew's hands onto the table. Jinx thought the silver spoon was the silver toy car! He knocked it from Princess's mouth, and it flew to the floor. Princess wanted to get the spoon, so she jumped to the floor.

Just then Jinx knocked the drum off the table. "Look out Princess, look out for the drum!" called Sally.

When Sally said, "drum," Rings jumped down on the floor. He started to hit the drum with his tail, faster and faster. But he hit Princess too! While Rings's tail flew,

Jinx jumped off the table. He wanted to get the silver spoon again. But this time he jumped on Rings.

Rings ran after Jinx! Princess ran after Rings!

Kevin watched the cats run around. Then he put his hands on his head. "That's the end of our show today. Thanks for watching!" he said.

And the TV show was over.